This journal belongs to:

- -

Welcome!

We are hoping this journal becomes one of your favorite parts of your *Come, Follow Me* study. In fact, we hope you will keep it right beside your scriptures and open it up every time you start to study. It's meant for taking notes and recording impressions. There are places to capture personal revelation as it comes and areas for you to think and process and reflect.

These pages are not simply meant for taking notes; it is our prayer that they will capture your journey this year, allowing you to have experiences and record your adventures as you come to know Jesus Christ better through the pages of the New Testament.

There is no wrong way to use this journal—instead, there is all of the potential in the world. Use watercolors, tape in favorite quotes, hand-letter your favorite verses. It's meant for deep learning and capturing the good parts and your most favorite things. By the time this year is over, we hope this journal will have become such an integral part of your learning process that you will treasure it forever.

Fill these pages up with everything you love about the New Testament we will too!

So grateful to be studying alongside you!

David & Emily

WHAT'S INCLUDED IN THIS JOURNAL...

1 DON'T MISS THIS DAILY

These five questions complement the *Don't Miss This* podcast and the YouTube videos. Maybe you will focus on one question each day Monday through Friday, or perhaps you will listen to the whole segment in one sitting and answer all of the questions at once. These questions might also be helpful to facilitate discussions in family or church lessons.

2 NOTES

Fill in these pages as you listen to each episode, answer the daily questions, prepare for your Sunday lessons, and participate in family discussions. Add quotes, use stickers, print out favorite social media posts. Be creative! We hope these pages become something you turn to regularly as a part of your daily scripture routine.

3 NAMES OF CHRIST

This year one of our focuses will be to study a name of Jesus Christ found in that week's study. Use this space to write down the name, ponder what it teaches you about the character of Christ, and consider how you have seen Him manifest that characteristic in your own story. Maybe you will look up other scripture verses that mention that name and write them in your notes as a resource for future talks or lessons.

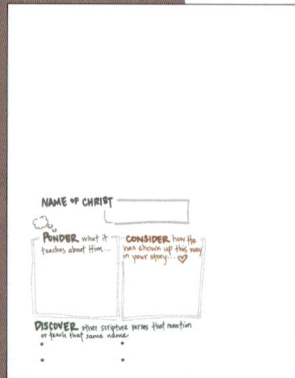

4 WORKBOOK PAGES

New this year! People ask us all the time if you were going to pick JUST ONE LESSON out of the weekly study to focus on, what would it be? So, the last page of each week will highlight ONE powerful lesson from the study with a colorful worksheet that you might use to help teach your family, your Sunday class, or to reinforce what you learn each week.

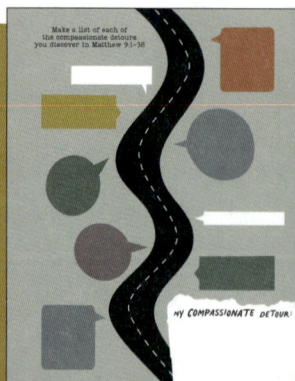

STUDY PLAN

FOR THE NEW TESTAMENT

Jan. 2–Jan. 8 ☐	Matthew 1; Luke 1
Jan. 9–Jan. 15 ☐	Matthew 2; Luke 2
Jan. 16–Jan. 22 ☐	John 1
Jan. 23–Jan. 29 ☐	Matthew 3; Mark 1; Luke 3
Jan. 30–Feb. 5 ☐	Matthew 4; Luke 4–5
Feb. 6–Feb. 12 ☐	John 2–4
Feb. 13–Feb. 19 ☐	Matthew 5; Luke 6
Feb. 20–Feb. 26 ☐	Matthew 6–7
Feb. 27–Mar. 5 ☐	Matthew 8; Mark 2–4; Luke 7
Mar. 6–Mar. 12 ☐	Matthew 9–10; Mark 5; Luke 9
Mar. 13–Mar. 19 ☐	Matthew 11–12; Luke 11
Mar. 20–Mar. 26 ☐	Matthew 13; Luke 8, 13
Mar. 27–Apr. 2 ☐	Matthew 14; Mark 6; John 5–6
Apr. 3–Apr. 9 ☐	Easter
Apr. 10–Apr. 16 ☐	Matthew 15–17; Mark 7–9
Apr. 17–Apr. 23 ☐	Matthew 18; Luke 10
Apr. 24–Apr. 30 ☐	John 7–10
May 1–May 7 ☐	Luke 12–17; John 11
May 8–May 14 ☐	Matthew 19-20; Mark 10; Luke 18
May 15–May 21 ☐	Matthew 21–23; Mark 11; Luke 19–20; John 12
May 22–May 28 ☐	JST, Matthew; Matthew 24–25; Mark 12–13; Luke 21
May 29–Jun. 4 ☐	Matthew 26; Mark 14; John 13
Jun. 5–Jun. 11 ☐	John 14–17
Jun. 12–Jun. 18 ☐	Luke 22; John 18
Jun. 19–Jun. 25 ☐	Matthew 27; Mark 15; Luke 23; John 19
Jun. 26–Jul. 2 ☐	Matthew 28; Mark 16; Luke 24; John 20–21
Jul. 3–Jul. 9 ☐	Acts 1–5
Jul. 10–Jul. 16 ☐	Acts 6–9
Jul. 17–Jul. 23 ☐	Acts 10–15
Jul. 24–Jul. 30 ☐	Acts 16–21
Jul. 31–Aug. 6 ☐	Acts 22–28
Aug. 7–Aug. 13 ☐	Romans 1–6
Aug. 14–Aug. 20 ☐	Romans 7–16
Aug. 21–Aug. 27 ☐	1 Corinthians 1–7
Aug. 28–Sep. 3 ☐	1 Corinthians 8–13
Sep. 4–Sep. 10 ☐	1 Corinthians 14–16
Sep. 11–Sep. 17 ☐	2 Corinthians 1–7
Sep. 18–Sep. 24 ☐	2 Corinthians 8–13
Sep. 25–Oct. 1 ☐	Galatians
Oct. 2–Oct. 8 ☐	Ephesians
Oct. 9–Oct. 15 ☐	Philippians; Colossians
Oct. 16–Oct. 22 ☐	1 and 2 Thessalonians
Oct. 23–Oct. 29 ☐	1 and 2 Timothy; Titus; Philemon
Oct. 30–Nov. 5 ☐	Hebrews 1–6
Nov. 6–Nov. 12 ☐	Hebrews 7–13
Nov. 13–Nov. 19 ☐	James
Nov. 20–Nov. 26 ☐	1 and 2 Peter
Nov. 27–Dec. 3 ☐	1, 2, and 3 John; Jude
Dec. 4–Dec. 10 ☐	Revelation 1–5
Dec. 11–Dec. 17 ☐	Revelation 6–14
Dec. 18–Dec. 24 ☐	Christmas
Dec. 25–Dec. 31 ☐	Revelation 15–22

1. Write what you remember or what you learned about the back story of each of the grandmothers of Christ found in Matthew 1:1–16.

- Tamar
- Rahab
- Bathsheba
- Ruth

This genealogy is less a line of who Jesus came through and more a reminder of who He came for. If this is who He came for, what do the grandmothers' stories teach us about the mission of Christ?

2. Each of the names for Jesus Christ teaches us something about who He is. What stands out to you about each of these names?

- Emmanuel (Matthew 1:23)
- Savior (Matthew 1:21)
- Jesus (Matthew 1:21)
- Christ (Matthew 1:16)

How has He been Emmanuel, Savior, Jesus, or the Christ in your story recently?

3. What was the two-word message from the angels to both Joseph and Mary? (Matthew 1:20; Luke 1:30). Where could you use that angelic advice in your life right now?

4. The story of Zacharias teaches five patterns to prepare us to better receive answers (Luke 1:1-20).

- Luke 1:6
- Luke 1:8
- Luke 1:9
- Luke 1:10
- Luke 1:20

5. The Gospel of Luke contains the stories of eyewitnesses (see Luke 1:1–2). In the opening chapter we meet some of the first eyewitnesses. What do you learn from the experience of each of these people?

- Elisabeth (Luke 1:40–45)
- Mary (Luke 1:46–55)
- Zacharias (Luke 1:67–79)

Things to
REMEMBER

NAME OF CHRIST

PONDER what it teaches about Him...

CONSIDER how He has shown up this way in your story... ♡

DISCOVER other scripture verses that mention or teach that same name

-
-

-
-

Mary's Psalm

And Mary said,

My soul doth magnify the Lord,

And my spirit hath rejoiced

in God my Saviour.

For he hath regarded the low estate

of his handmaiden:

for, behold,

from henceforth

all generations shall call me blessed.

For he that is mighty

hath done to me great things;

and holy is his name.

And his mercy

is on them that fear him

from generation to generation.

He hath shewed

strength with his arm;

he hath scattered the proud

in the imagination of their hearts.

He hath put down the mighty

from their seats,

and exalted them of low degree.

He hath filled the hungry

with good things;

and the rich he hath sent empty away.

He hath holpen his servant Israel,

in remembrance of his mercy;

As he spake to our fathers, to Abraham,

and to his seed for ever.

Luke 1:46—55

1. Imagine what it would have been like to have witnessed the very first Christmas. What do you want to remember from each of the stories of those who were there? (Luke 2).

- Mary and Joseph (Luke 2:4–7, 16–19)

- Shepherds (Luke 2:8–9, 15–18, 20)

- Angels (Luke 2:10–14)

- Wise men (Matthew 2:9–12)

- Simeon and Anna (Luke 2:25–38)

2. We don't have many verses that tell us about Jesus as a child. What do you learn about Him from Luke 2:40?

A place for thoughts...

NAME OF CHRIST

PONDER what it teaches about Him...

CONSIDER how He has shown up this way in your story... ♡

DISCOVER other scripture verses that mention or teach that same name

-
-

-
-

Encounters

WITH
Jesus

MARY

JOSEPH

What did each of these people learn from their encounter with Christ?

LUKE 2

ANGELS

SHEPHERDS

WISE MEN

ANNA

SIMEON

1. What do you learn from John's introduction of Jesus Christ about His life, character, and mission? (John 1:1–18).

- How is He the word?

- How is He light?

- How is He life?

2. What three things does John teach that should be part of our process of becoming? "But as many as _____ him, to them gave he _____ to become the sons of God, even to them that _____ on his name" (John 1:12). Is this you? What do we learn from v. 16 that is also important to this process?

3. One important question you might ask yourself as you enter into relationship with Jesus Christ is, "What seek ye?" (John 1:37). How would you answer that question? What are you looking for?

4. Who were each of these people seeking?

- John the Baptist (John 1:36)

- Andrew to Simon Peter (John 1:41)

- Philip (John 1:45)

- Nathanael (John 1:49)

5. What are some of the great things you have seen as you have invited Jesus into your story? What are some of the things you are looking forward to? (John 1:50).

CURRENTLY
THINKING
ABOUT

NAME OF CHRIST

PONDER what it teaches about Him...

CONSIDER how He has shown up this way in your story... ♡

DISCOVER other scripture verses that mention or teach that same name

-
-

-
-

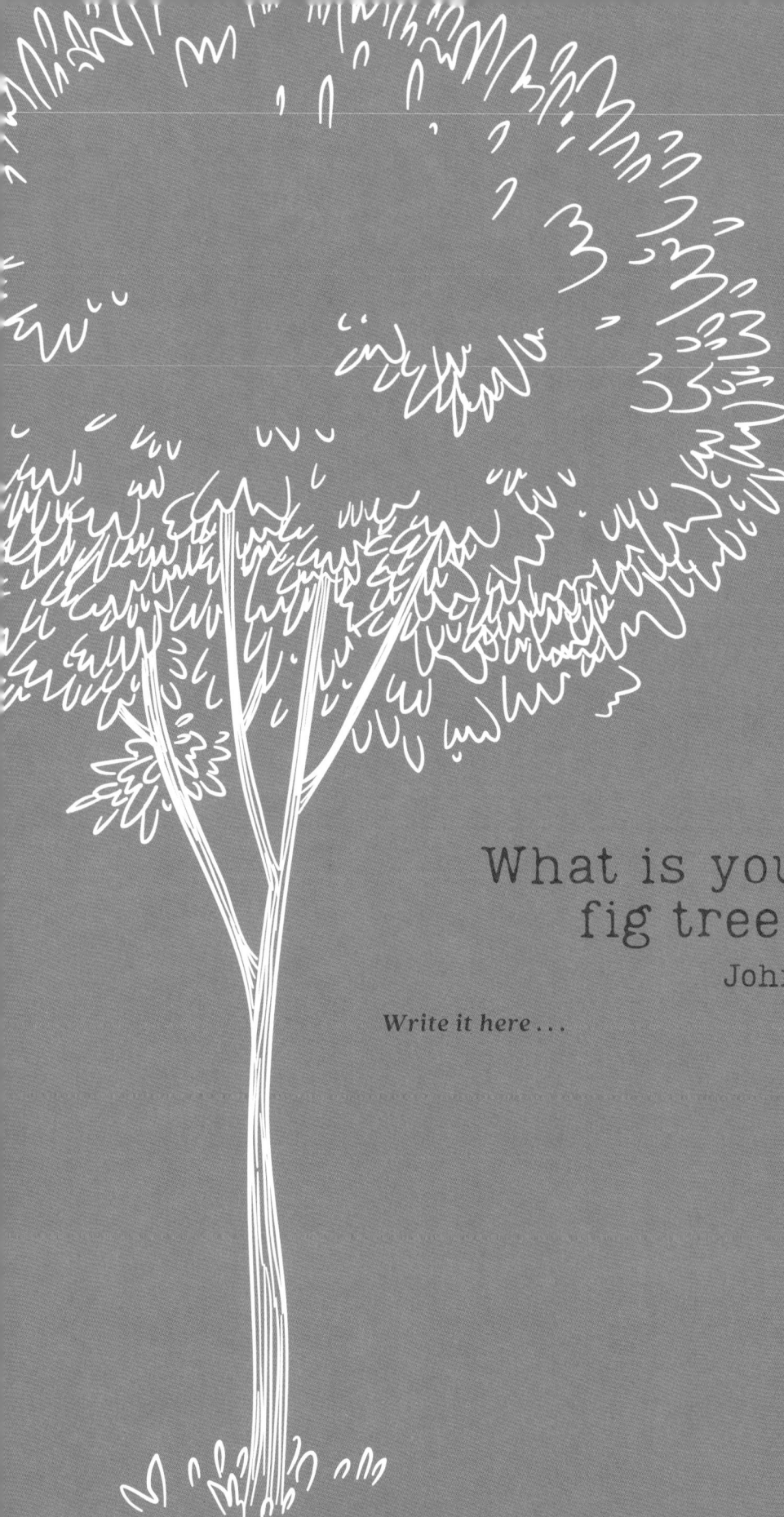

What is your
fig tree moment?

John 1:48

Write it here . . .

1. What have your own wilderness places taught you about the ways of the Lord? (Matthew 3:3).

2. What do you learn about how the Father felt about Christ before His mission even began? (Matthew 3:17).

- my

- beloved

- Son

- well pleased

3. What could the Lord make you to become? (Mark 1:17).

4. What does Christ's routine teach you about shaping your morning? (Mark 1:35–38). Do you have a solitary place?

5. Consider your life—the empty places, the rough patches. What do you learn from the people asking the question, "What should I do?" in Luke 3:4–14? What advice do you think He would give you if you asked the same question regarding your life right now?

MEMORABLE

NAME OF CHRIST

PONDER what it
teaches about Him...

CONSIDER how He
has shown up this way
in your story... ♡

DISCOVER other scripture verses that mention
or teach that same name

- •

- •

- •

- •

CHANGING THE SHAPE OF MY DAY

MARK 1:17

- What does God believe about me?

- What will He make me to become?

- Where should I GO today?

- Whom should I SERVE today?

- What shall I DO today?

(See Dieter F. Uchtdorf, "Daily Restoration," *Liahona*, November 2021, 77–79.)

1. Did you notice how Jesus answered every temptation from Satan with an answer from the scriptures? (Matthew 4:4, 7, 10). Those answers became protection for Him against the attacks of the adversary. What is your protection scripture for times of trouble?

2. The undermining and underlying attack in this chapter from the adversary is focused on the identity of Jesus:

   • *If* you are the Son of God (Matthew 4:3).
   • *If* you are the Son of God (Matthew 4:6).

What does Jesus already know about who He is and where did He learn it? (Matthew 3:17). What do you already know about who you are? Where did you learn it?

3. Read Luke 4:18–19. What did Jesus say He came to do? Then read Luke 4:21. Try to remember a time when this scripture was fulfilled for you. When has He come into your story in similar ways?

4. In Luke 4 we read about two groups of people—belief dashers and miracle seekers. What do those who choose to believe discover about a life invested in Christ? (Luke 4:40–43). What has your experience been when you have chosen to believe?

5. In Luke 5:6–7 we read about boats sinking with blessings and nets breaking with goodness. When has that happened for you?

what is filling up my heart

NAME OF CHRIST [_____]

PONDER what it teaches about Him...

CONSIDER how He has shown up this way in your story... ♡

DISCOVER other scripture verses that mention or teach that same name

- •
- •
- •
- •

How could you . . .

THRUST OUT A LITTLE

LAUNCH OUT INTO THE DEEP

LET DOWN YOUR NETS

LEAVE BEHIND YOUR NETS

FOLLOW ME

The Invitations Jesus Gave to Peter in Luke 5

1. In the story of the water turned to wine, Jesus saw something ordinary and envisioned what it could be. When have you experienced what seemed like a "thrift shop miracle"? (John 2:1–12). When has He taken something ordinary and turned it into something extraordinary?

2. Nicodemus

   • What did he know? (John 3:2).

   • What was he asking? (John 3:9, 12).

   • What did he learn? (John 3:16).

3. Woman at the well

   • What did she know? (John 4:25).

   • What was she asking? (John 4:11–12).

   • What did she learn? (John 4:26).

4. From these three stories we see how Jesus meets you where you are, as you are—behind the scenes, in the darkest of nights or in the ordinary tasks of your days. When has He met you where you were and as you were to answer your questions?

5. Jesus did not intend to leave any of these people in the place where they were. He saw ordinary water and turned it into wine. He offered Nicodemus a new way of life—to be born again. He offered the woman at the well more than just a drink of water—instead, a well of water springing up unto everlasting life. Where do you see change and the potential for new life happening in you?

everything
I'm soaking in

NAME OF CHRIST

PONDER what it teaches about Him...

CONSIDER how He has shown up this way in your story... ♡

DISCOVER other scripture verses that mention or teach that same name

-
-
-
-

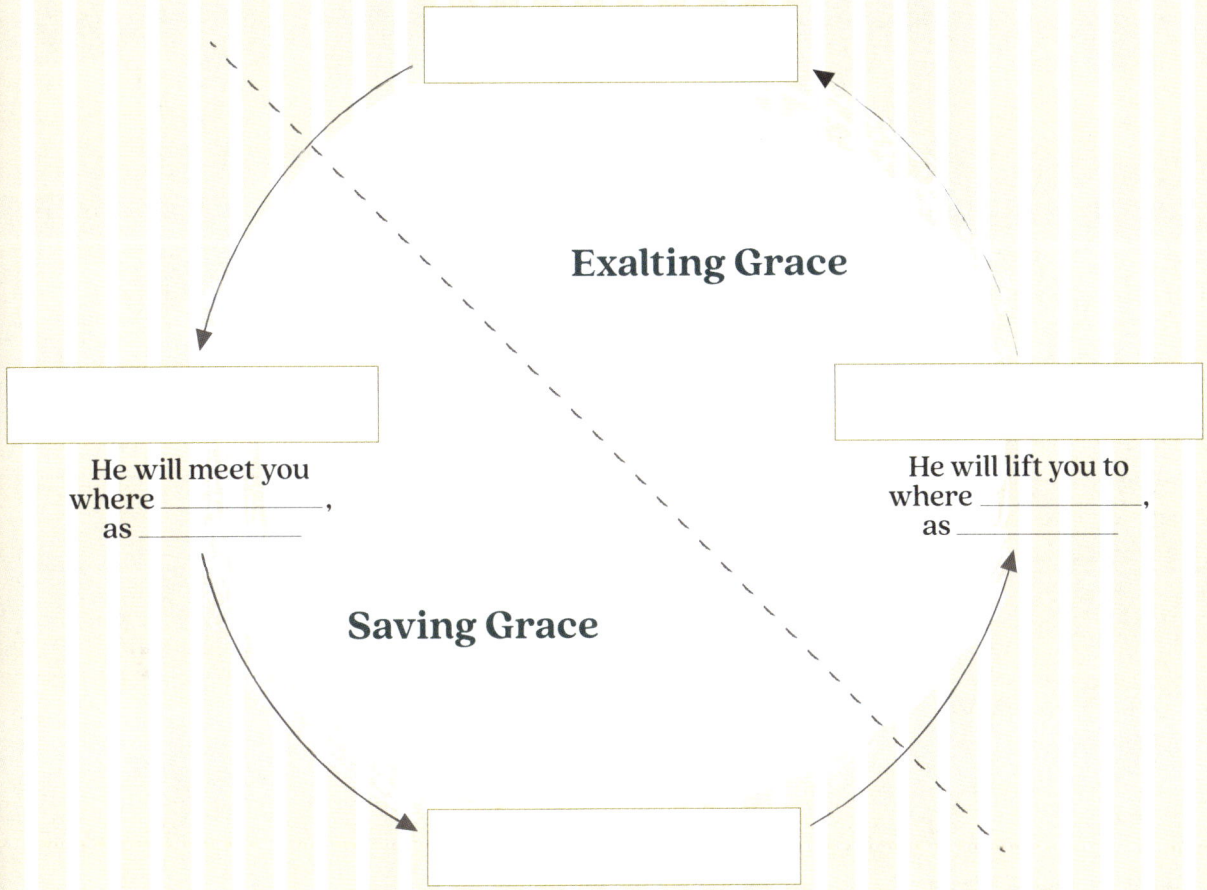

Exalting Grace

He will meet you where _____,
as _____

He will lift you to where _____,
as _____

Saving Grace

1. Read Matthew 5:1.

And seeing the _____, he went _____ into a _____: and when he was _____, his _____ came _____ him.

This is the first verse of the Sermon on the Mount. What if this was the only verse we had for the Sermon on the Mount? What message do you think Jesus was trying to teach?

The last verse (Matthew 5:48) is just as important to the sermon. Look in the footnote for the Greek translation of "perfect" _____, _____. _____. What is Jesus teaching about the process of becoming?

2. James E. Talmage taught that Matthew 5:2–12 was a discourse on what constitutes genuine blessedness. Where do you see Beatitude-style blessedness in your own life right now?

3. Name some outward expressions of inward commitments.

4. Read Matthew 5:17–48 and describe what you imagine discipleship looks like.

5. Read Luke 6:38, 48. What do you learn about good measure and digging deep?

INSIGHTS & Impressions

NAME OF CHRIST

PONDER what it teaches about Him...

CONSIDER how He has shown up this way in your story... ♡

DISCOVER other scripture verses that mention or teach that same name
-
-
-
-

When you feel you are lacking
you are blessed because

....

....

....

When you become content where you are
you are blessed because

....

....

....

When you offer your heart to someone in need
you are blessed because

....

....

....

When your heart is broken
you are blessed because

....

....

....

THE HAPPINESS CODE

(SEE MATTHEW 5:3-12)

When you seek for the good
you are blessed because

....

....

....

When you are empty and unsatisfied
you are blessed because

....

....

....

When your relationships need reconciliation
you are blessed because

....

....

....

When you feel like you don't belong
you are blessed because

....

....

....

1. One of the things we learn from the Lord's Prayer in Matthew 6:9–15 is the power of one-word prayers. Here we see words such as *give, forgive, deliver,* and *come.* Consider each one.

What do you need Him to
GIVE _____
FORGIVE _____

How might He
DELIVER _____
COME _____

What are some one-word prayers you have spoken?

2. Have you ever received an answer that seemed like a stone but you later learned it was bread? (Matthew 7:7–11). What did you learn from that experience?

3. When we consider the lilies, we are reminded how God clothes desert places with beautiful things. What have been some of your lilies of the field? (Matthew 6:28–30).

4. Which of the object lessons found in the Sermon on the Mount speaks to you the most in your life right now? Why?

5. What are the treasures that fill your life because of the gospel of Jesus Christ? What things have been added to your life because of Him?

inspiration

NAME OF CHRIST [_____]

PONDER what it teaches about Him...

CONSIDER how He has shown up this way in your story... ♡

DISCOVER other scripture verses that mention or teach that same name
-
-
-
-

Find objects in your house **to represent** each of these verses.

Attach one of these scriptures to each object you find.

See Matthew 5–7

☐ CUT IT OUT
Matthew 5:29–30

☐ GO A MILE
Matthew 5:40–41

☐ TREASURE
Matthew 6:19–21

☐ THE LIGHT OF THE BODY
Matthew 6:22

☐ CONSIDER THE LILIES
Matthew 6:26–30

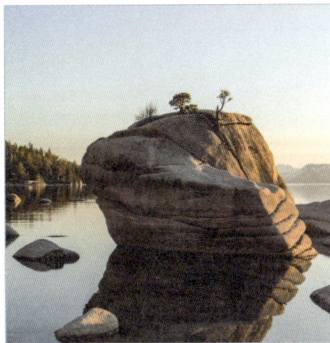

☐ HOUSE ON THE ROCK
Matthew 7:24–27

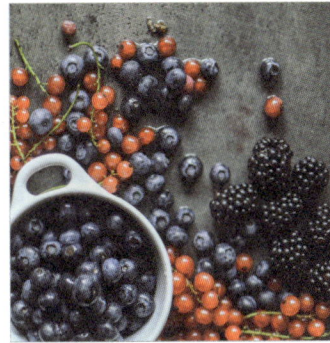

☐ BY THEIR FRUITS YE SHALL KNOW THEM
Matthew 7:17–20

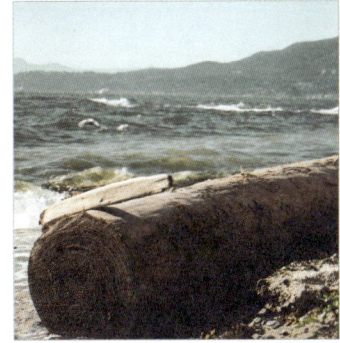

☐ BEAM IN YOUR EYE
Matthew 7:1–5

☐ PEARLS BEFORE SWINE
Matthew 7:6

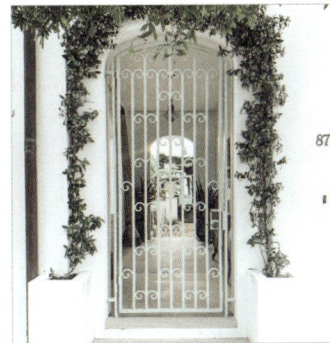

☐ THE STRAIT GATE
Matthew 7:13–14

☐ WOLVES IN SHEEP'S CLOTHING
Matthew 7:15–16

1. If Matthew 8:1–4 was the only story you knew about Jesus, what would you know?

2. From the centurion in Luke 7:1–10, we learn that sometimes what we see in ourselves is less than what Jesus sees in us. What do you think He would find "so great" in you?

3. In what ways do you believe Jesus has recognized your fear and then strengthened your faith? (Matthew 8:24–27).

4. When the friends came to Jesus what He acknowledged first was _____ faith (Mark 2:5). Do you have a friend whose faith has had an impact on your healing or spiritual wholeness? How?

5. Read Luke 7:47. What reason do you have to love much?

Reflections

NAME OF CHRIST

PONDER what it teaches about Him...

CONSIDER how He has shown up this way in your story... ♡

DISCOVER other scripture verses that mention or teach that same name
-
-
-
-

Here are some of the lessons we learn from the four friends in Mark 2 who brought their friend to Christ. How could you do the same?

GO AFTER THE ONE.

_____

BRING OTHERS ALONG.

_____

HELP BEAR THE BURDEN.

_____

GO TO EXTRAORDINARY MEASURES.

_____

HAVE FAITH.

_____

TESTIFY OF WHO HE IS.

_____

Let God be God—
don't get in
the way of
the miracle...

1. It seems that Jesus gave some of His disciples nicknames representing their good qualities or who they might become. What were His nicknames for the people below?

- Simon (Matthew 10:2) _____
- Nathanael (John 1:47) _____
- James and John (Mark 3:17) _____

What might His nickname be for you?

2. Consider the woman who touched Christ's robe.

- How long had she been sick? (Mark 5:25).

- What had she tried? (Mark 5:26).

- How quickly did the healing come? (Mark 5:29–30).

What do you learn from her waiting and trying, and then finally the healing? We learn that it was her faith that made her whole. Do you wonder what might have happened in the waiting that contributed to her faith in that moment? What have you learned in the waiting?

3. What impact do you think seeing the woman with the issue of blood healed had on Jairus's faith? When have you witnessed something miraculous that has increased your faith? (Mark 5:36).

4. What is the first question that Jesus asks the man of the Gadarenes? (Mark 5:9; Luke 8:30). Why is that so significant? Does that change how you think He would approach you?

5. What do you think it means to be "moved with compassion"? (Matthew 9:36).

NAME OF CHRIST ⌐_____⌐

PONDER what it teaches about Him...

CONSIDER how He has shown up this way in your story... ♡

DISCOVER other scripture verses that mention or teach that same name

-
-
-
-

Make a list of each of the compassionate detours you discover in Matthew 9:1-38.

MY COMPASSIONATE DETOUR:

1. Sometimes we experience times of doubt or discouragement. What are you HEARING and SEEING that reminds you that God is at work? (Matthew 11:3—5).

2. Consider comparing the yoke Jesus asks us to take upon ourselves to spiritual rhythms that include Him. What are some spiritual rhythms you have embraced that give you rest? (Matthew 11:28—30).

3. In Greek, *Sabbath* means a day of repose, and in Hebrew it means an intermission. What does it mean to you to live in Sabbath? (Matthew 12:1—13).

4. "And it came to pass, that, as he was _____ in a certain place, when he ceased, one of his disciples said unto him, Lord, teach us to _____ " (Luke 11:1). Have you invited the Lord into your day to day life—including into your mistakes and messes, into your weakness, into your battles, and into your midnight hours? How did He respond?

5. Read Luke 9:62 along with Luke 11:34—36. What do you have your eye set on, and what impact is that having on you right now?

discoveries

NAME OF CHRIST [_____]

PONDER what it teaches about Him...

CONSIDER how He has shown up this way in your story... ♡

DISCOVER other scripture verses that mention or teach that same name
-
-
-
-

PLAN YOUR SABBATH

Add activities to each quadrant of your Sabbath path that will help you find a place with God, rest, loved ones, and prayer.

GOD

PRAYER

LIVING IN SABBATH

REST

LOVED ONES

Here are some things you could consider adding: songs that remind me of God; songs that remind me of Jesus; food I will eat; what I will wear to church; meditation or other uplifting traditions for the day; people I will visit; inspirational reading I will do; where to go for a walk.

1. Why does the Lord speak in parables? (See the Bible Dictionary, "Parables.") Read Matthew 13:15. Parables help you _____ , _____ , _____ , _____ and be _____ .

Has He used something ordinary in your life to teach you a lesson? What "parable" from your everyday life could you share?

2. Read the parable of the sower (Matthew 13:4–8). Describe the condition of the soil in each of the circumstances. How does that compare to the condition of a heart? How would you describe your heart?

3. Notice that the Lord begins each of these parables with the same phrase, "The kingdom of heaven is like . . ." What do you think Jesus is trying to show us about the kingdom of heaven from

- the wheat and tares (Matthew 13:24–30)?

- the big tree (Matthew 13:31–32)?

- leaven (Matthew 13:33)?

4. What do you learn about the kingdom of heaven from

- the treasure (Matthew 13:44)?

- the pearl (Matthew 13:45–46)?

- the net (Matthew 13:47–48)?

5. At the beginning of Luke 8, we read about three women from different backgrounds who were with Christ. Who were they?

-

-

-

They ministered unto Him of their _____ . What is your substance?

So good

NAME OF CHRIST

PONDER what it teaches about Him...

CONSIDER how He has shown up this way in your story... ♡

DISCOVER other scripture verses that mention or teach that same name

-
-

-
-

PARABLE PRACTICE

Matthew 13

Draw each of these parables

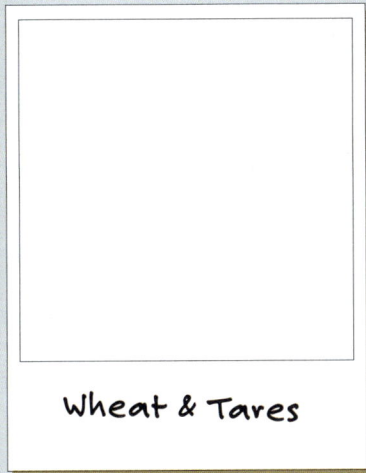

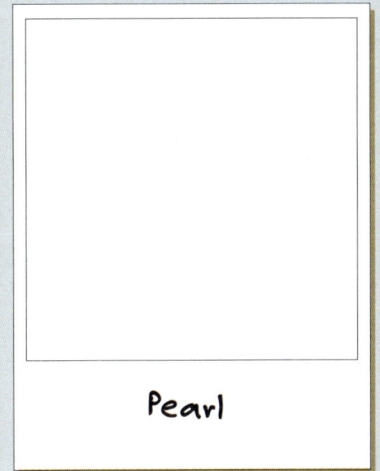

Sower

Wheat & Tares

Treasure

Pearl

Net

Mustard Tree

Leaven

1. You don't have to be someone "well known" to make a difference. Have you ever considered that perhaps it was the woman who touched Christ's robe that made a difference to the people in Mark 6:56? We don't even know her name. Maybe her witness was the catalyst of faith for others to also be healed. Whose story, including those from the scriptures, has encouraged your faith? (John 5:39).

2. In the story of Peter walking on water, what do we learn we can expect from Jesus? (Matthew 14:24–33).

3. In the story of the man at Bethesda, what do we learn we can expect from Jesus? (John 5:1–9).

4. In the story of feeding the 5,000, what do we learn we can expect from Jesus? (John 6:1–14).

5. After considering each of those stories, how would you have answered the question in John 6:67, "Will you also go away?" Why would you choose to stay?

A THING
OR TWO
I'VE LEARNED

NAME OF CHRIST [_____]

PONDER what it teaches about Him...

CONSIDER how He has shown up this way in your story... ♡

DISCOVER other scripture verses that mention or teach that same name

-
-
-
-

Progressing in Jesus

FEAR   Matthew 14:26

WHAT DID PETER FEAR? _____

WHAT DO I? _____

STRETCHING   Matthew 14:28

HOW DID PETER STRETCH? _____

HOW WILL I? _____

SUCCESS   Matthew 14:29

WHAT WAS PETER'S SUCCESS? _____

WHAT IS MINE? _____

DOUBT   Matthew 14:30

WHY DID PETER DOUBT? _____

WHY DO I? _____

SAVING GRACE   Matthew 14:31

HOW DID PETER EXPERIENCE SAVING GRACE? _____

HOW DO I? _____

TESTIMONY   Matthew 14:33

WHAT WAS PETER'S TESTIMONY OF CHRIST? _____

WHAT IS MINE? _____

What do you find significant about this order?

What does it teach you about progressing?

dontmissthisstudy.com

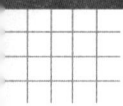

THINGS
TO PAY
ATTENTION TO

NAME OF CHRIST [_____]

PONDER what it teaches about Him...

CONSIDER how He has shown up this way in your story... ♡

DISCOVER other scripture verses that mention or teach that same name
- .
- .

- .
- .

1. Have you ever had a single-loaf moment, when you forgot what the Lord was capable of doing? How did He remind you? (Mark 8:18—21).

2. When have you been content with the crumbs? When has the Lord offered you a whole meal? (Matthew 15:27—28).

3. When have you had a Caesarea Philippi moment? (Matthew 16:15—19). When have you had a must-go-to-Jerusalem moment? (Matthew 16:21—23). When have you had a collecting-the-coins moment? (Matthew 17:24—27).

4. Have you experienced healing in stages, or do you know someone who has? (Mark 8:23—24). Why do you think the Lord sometimes chooses to heal in this way?

5. When you consider your burdens, you might feel lost in the multitude, and yet He is capable of recognizing the one. When has He had compassion on you? When has He recognized you? When has He helped you believe? (Mark 9:17—29).

*write
that
down!*

NAME OF CHRIST

PONDER what it teaches about Him...

CONSIDER how He has shown up this way in your story... ♡

DISCOVER other scripture verses that mention or teach that same name
-
-
-
-

Read Mark 7:31-35

Read Mark 8:22-25

1

HOW DOES HE REMOVE THE DISTRACTION?

1

HOW DOES HE REMOVE THE DISTRACTION?

2

HOW DOES HE ENTER THIS STORY IN UNCOMFORTABLE AND UNPREDICTABLE WAYS?

2

HOW DOES HE ENTER THIS STORY IN UNCOMFORTABLE AND UNPREDICTABLE WAYS?

3

HOW DOES HE INVITE HIM TO CHANGE HIS PERSPECTIVE?

3

HOW DOES HE INVITE HIM TO CHANGE HIS PERSPECTIVE?

HOW WOULD YOU HAVE RESPONDED?

1. The amount of 10,000 talents was intended to be beyond calculation, the largest possible amount. What is Jesus saying about your worth if He is willing to make that kind of investment in your behalf? (Matthew 18:23–33).

2. Jesus intends us to be a community of disciples. Our relationship with others becomes as important as our relationship with the Lord. What kind of conversations or experiences with two or three have allowed you to feel His presence? How were they similar to or different from your solitary moments with Him? (Matthew 18:19–20).

3. Read Luke 10:38–42. What do you learn about Mary? What do you learn about Martha? Read John 11:19–27. What do you learn about Martha? What do you learn about Mary? What does this teach you about choosing the good part?

4. What do you learn about grace and the Atonement of Jesus Christ from the Parable of the Good Samaritan? (Luke 10:29–37).

5. What do you learn about *creating the inn* from the Parable of the Good Samaritan? (Luke 10:29–37, especially v. 35).

Things I don't want to forget . . .

NAME OF CHRIST

PONDER what it teaches about Him...

CONSIDER how He has shown up this way in your story... ♡

DISCOVER other scripture verses that mention or teach that same name

-
-

PROVIDE A PLACE OF SAFETY
refuge, rest, healing, grace

How can I?

TAKE CARE OF HIM
clean or unclean
Samaritan or Jew
come as you are

How can I?

BE
THE
INN

Luke 10:25–37

SPEND MORE
it's going to cost you something
through the night
bear the burden
be a host

How can I?

GO AND DO THOU LIKEWISE

How can I?

dontmissthisstudy.com

Sometimes questions become the most powerful part of a learning experience. It is often true in scripture. Consider these questions found in this week's reading. How were they answered? What is the lesson found in the asking and answering of each of these?

1. "Art thou also of Galilee?" (John 7:52).

2. "Who art thou?" (John 8:25).

3. "Are we blind also?" (John 9:40).

4. "How long do you make us doubt?" (John 10:24).

5. "For which of these works do you stone me?" (John 10:32).

Things to
REMEMBER

NAME OF CHRIST

PONDER what it teaches about Him...

CONSIDER how He has shown up this way in your story... ♡

DISCOVER other scripture verses that mention or teach that same name

-
-
-
-

What does a shepherd do?

JOHN 10:1-18 & 27 —— PSALM 23

Where do you see Christ
shepherding you?

1. What might radical generosity look like in your life? (Luke 14:16—24).

2. What is similar about the three parables of the lost sheep, the lost coin, and the lost boy? (Luke 15:4—32).

- one

- until (till)

- found

- rejoice

3. Put yourself in the shoes of each of the characters in the Parable of the Prodigal Son (Luke 15:11—32). What do you learn from each?

- the younger son

- the elder son

- the father

4. What does it look like to live like the last leper? (Luke 17:11—19).

1.
2.
3.
4.
5.
6.
7.

5. When has the Lord called you to come forth out of a dark place to be healed? (John 11:43).

A
place
for
thoughts...

NAME OF CHRIST

PONDER what it teaches about Him...

CONSIDER how He has shown up this way in your story... ♡

DISCOVER other scripture verses that mention or teach that same name

-
-
-
-

COME TO THE TABLE

LUKE 14:16-24

WHO WAS INVITED	WHAT HELD THEM BACK	HOW THEY GOT THERE
The man with the piece of ground		
The man with the new wife		
The man with the oxen		
The poor		
The maimed		
The halt		
The blind		
Those on the highway		
Those in the hedges		

WHAT WAS HE SERVING:

dontmissthisstudy.com

1. Read Luke 18:1—8 and Luke 18:35—43, two bookends on how to pray and to not faint. When have you "cried so much the more" and how did the Lord respond?

2. Rich people are often accustomed to earning and deserving their end reward. Jesus says it will be harder for them to get into heaven. Why? Perhaps it is because earning their own way is their only perspective. What does the rich young ruler need to learn about being saved? (Mark 10:17—27).

3. Read Mark 10:21, "Then Jesus _____ him _____ him. Sometimes Jesus will ask us to do hard things even though He loves us—perhaps *because* He loves us. What is He trying to teach us by asking us to do the hard thing? In reality, where is our lack?

4. Read Luke 18:10—17. What is the difference between checklist living and heartfelt submission? What paves the road to exaltation?

5. Read Matthew 20:1—16. This is not a parable about _____ : this is a parable about _____ . What does the penny represent? How have you experienced God's pennies lately?

NAME OF CHRIST

PONDER what it teaches about Him...

CONSIDER how He has shown up this way in your story... ♡

DISCOVER other scripture verses that mention or teach that same name

-
-

-
-

THE PENNY PARABLE

Matthew 20:1–15

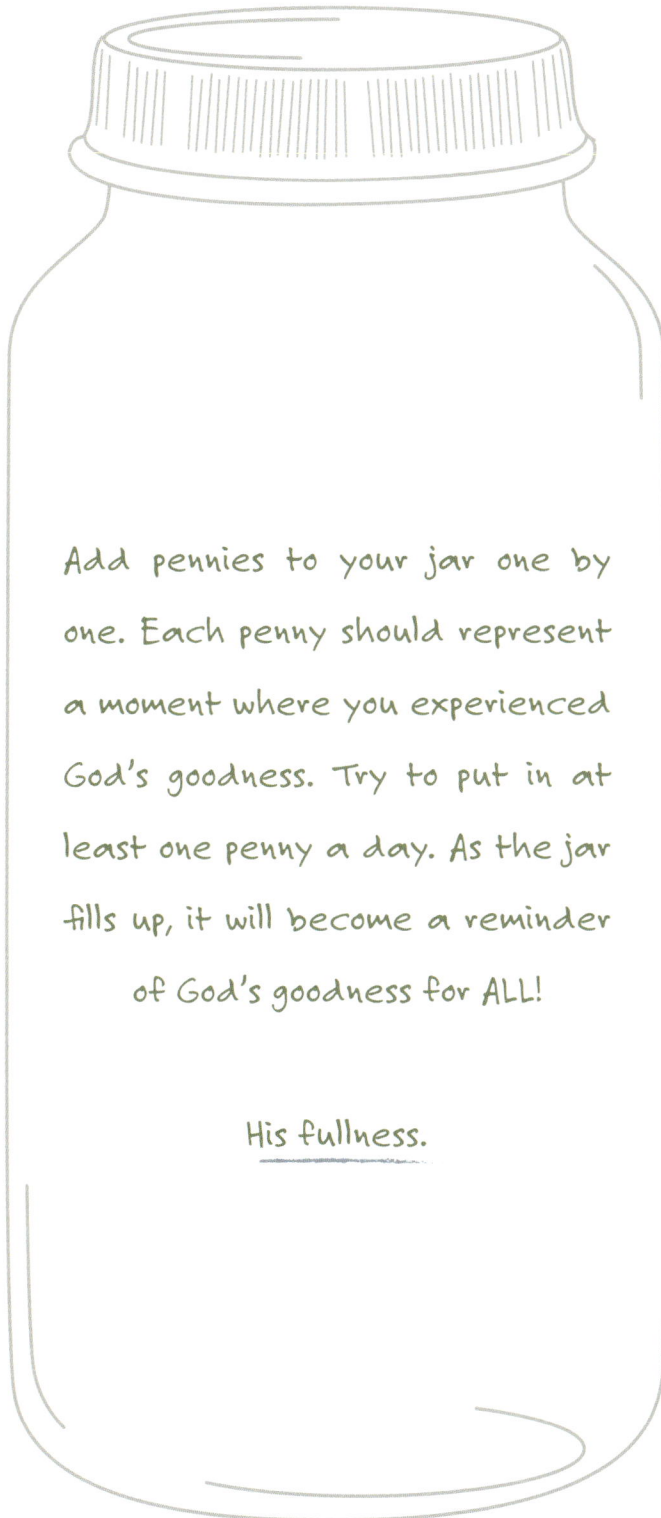

Add pennies to your jar one by one. Each penny should represent a moment where you experienced God's goodness. Try to put in at least one penny a day. As the jar fills up, it will become a reminder of God's goodness for ALL!

His fullness.

They received every man a penny! Friend, did you not agree with me for a penny? Because I am good. A penny = the goodness of God. ALL that the Father has in this hour! Experience God's goodness. Goodness for ALL!

1. *Hosanna* can be a cry of adoration, a plea for help, or a cry for salvation. It also is used at times to express gratitude. If you had been in the crowd that gathered for the triumphal entry (Matthew 21:1–11; Mark 11:1–11; Luke 19:28–44; John 12:12–19), which hosanna would you have shouted?

2. What do you learn about a God who keeps on trying when you read the parable in Matthew 21:33–46? How have you seen God show up?

3. Do you remember a moment in your life where things were taken away or turned upside down and it made room for the healing only Jesus can bring? (Matthew 21:12, 19).

4. Love _____ . Love _____ .
"On these two commandments hang all the law and the prophets" (Matthew 22:37–40). Read Matthew 21:2–3; Mark 11:4–5. How does the story of the colt show you what love for God looks like? When two ways meet, how does love for God define your response?

5. Read Luke 19:1–10. Watch how Jesus shows love for Zacchaeus. What do you notice? How does that help you know how to show love for others in the same way that He would?

MEMORABLE

NAME OF CHRIST

PONDER what it
teaches about Him...

CONSIDER how He
has shown up this way
in your story... ♡

DISCOVER other scripture verses that mention
or teach that same name
-
-

LOVE GOD

MARK 11:1-10

LOVE PEOPLE

LUKE 19:1-10

Thou shalt love the Lord thy God with all thy heart . . .
thou shalt love thy neighbour as thyself . . .
on these two commandments hang all . . .

MATTHEW 22:36-40

1. What part does revelation play in preparing you for the last days? What particular revelations from Matthew 24 or recent general conferences are helping you navigate?

2. What spiritual practices are helping you add oil to your lamp? (Matthew 25:1–13).

3. Where are you experiencing spiritual increase or progression? (Matthew 25:14–30).

4. Jesus taught us that when we see and love others in need, we are seeing and loving Him. When have you "seen" the Lord lately? How did you respond?

5. When has the Savior met you in the treasury? When has He seen your falling short? How did He respond? (Mark 12:41–44).

So good

NAME OF CHRIST

PONDER what it teaches about Him...

CONSIDER how He has shown up this way in your story... ♡

DISCOVER other scripture verses that mention or teach that same name

-
-

-
-

THE THREE PARABLES

	VIRGINS *Matt. 25:1–13*	TALENTS *Matt. 25:14–29*	GOATS *Matt. 25:31–45*	ME
What did the waiting look like?				
Describe the moment of decision.				
What were they entrusted with?				
What did they know about the Lord?				

1. When was the last time you broke open the alabaster box? (Mark 14:3−9). When have you given up something for Him at great cost to yourself?

2. What is the significance of the elements of the first Passover meal?

- Bitter herbs

- Unleavened bread

- Cups of wine

- The lamb

3. On the night of the Last Supper, how does Jesus change the significance of the Passover story and meal moving forward? (Mark 14:22−25).

4. How does the story of the Passover and the Last Supper change the way you view your sacrament experience?

5. Consider the story of Jesus washing Peter's feet. How do you think you would respond if you were Peter? What do you learn about letting Jesus love you? (John 13:1−17).

everything
  I'm soaking in

NAME OF CHRIST _____

PONDER what it teaches about Him...

CONSIDER how He has shown up this way in your story... ♡

DISCOVER other scripture verses that mention or teach that same name

-
-

-
-

WHEN HAVE YOU BROKEN OPEN THE ALABASTER BOX? (MARK 14:3-9)

What was the cost?

1. Why does true friendship require love? (John 14:15; 15:13—17).

2. How does the Holy Ghost bring comfort? (John 14:16).

3. What does Jesus teach us about how to remain cheerful in times of tribulation? (John 16:13—20, 33).

4. What does the analogy of the vine and the branch teach you about staying connected to and abiding in Him? (John 14:6; 15:1—9). What do you think that would look like in real life?

5. What does the relationship between the Son and the Father teach you about being one? (John 17).

THINGS TO
PAY ATTENTION TO

NAME OF CHRIST

PONDER what it teaches about Him...

CONSIDER how He has shown up this way in your story... ♡

DISCOVER other scripture verses that mention or teach that same name

-
-
-
-

WHAT DOES IT LOOK LIKE TO . . .

LOVE

COMFORT

CHEER

ABIDE

BE ONE

----

1. How did the angel strengthen? (Luke 22:41—44).

2. Why do you think Judas betrayed? (John 18:1—5; Luke 22:47—48).

3. What do you think Malchus wondered? (John 18:10; Luke 22:50—51).

4. Why do you think Pilate compromised? (John 18:28—40).

5. What process led to Peter's conversion? (Luke 22:31—34).

inspiration

NAME OF CHRIST

PONDER what it teaches about Him...

CONSIDER how He has shown up this way in your story... ♡

DISCOVER other scripture verses that mention or teach that same name
- ●
- ●
- ●
- ●

IN CRITICAL MOMENTS
HOW DID THEY RESPOND?

The angel strengthens Luke 22:41–44

Judas betrays Luke 22:47–48

Malchus wonders Luke 22:50–51; John 18:10

Pilate compromises John 18:29, 32–38

Peter becomes converted Luke 22:31–32, 54–62

How would you?

1. What do you learn from Simon who carried the cross? (Mark 15:21).

2. What do you learn from the women who ministered? (John 19:25−27; Matthew 27:55−56).

3. What do you learn from the centurion who believed? (Matthew 27:50−54).

4. What do you learn from the way Jesus gives hope to the thieves? (Luke 23:39−43).

5. What do you learn from how Nicodemus changed? (John 19:38−41; Matthew 27:58).

Things I don't
want to forget . . .

NAME OF CHRIST [_____]

PONDER what it teaches about Him...

CONSIDER how He has shown up this way in your story... ♡

DISCOVER other scripture verses that mention or teach that same name
-
-
-
-

IN CRITICAL MOMENTS
HOW DID THEY RESPOND?

Simon carried Mark 15:20–22

The women ministered Matthew 27:55–56

The centurion believed Mark 15:39

Jesus gives hope Luke 23:39–43

Joseph and Nicodemus risk everything John 19:38–41

How would you?

1. How does Jesus acknowledge Thomas's doubt? How does He respond to it? (John 20:24–29).

2. When have you missed Christ in a present moment and then looked back and realized He was there all along? (Luke 24:32).

3. When has Jesus taken a moment of weeping and given you hope? (John 20:11–16).

4. When Jesus met the apostles by the Sea of Galilee and filled their nets, someone took time to count the fish—to remember the miracles hadn't ceased. Take some time to count your fish and record them here (John 21:1–11).

5. Read the last few verses of every gospel. What is the final departing message of each one?

CURRENTLY THINKING ABOUT

NAME OF CHRIST

PONDER what it teaches about Him...

CONSIDER how He has shown up this way in your story... ♡

DISCOVER other scripture verses that mention or teach that same name

-
-

-
-

and there were also many other things which Jesus did . . .

- Looking back over the whole of the Gospels, which was your favorite story of Jesus?

and it came to pass . . .

- Where has He shown up in your own story?
  John 21:25

1. Where have you seen Jesus show up in your story? How might those moments become "infallible proofs" of His reality? (Acts 1:3).

2. In Acts 2 we read several descriptions of the Spirit. Which would you pick as your favorite? What does the Spirit feel like to you?

3. As you watch Peter's actions with the lame man, what do you think he had learned from his few years watching Jesus? (Acts 3:1–11).

4. What was it that filled the people "with wonder and amazement"? (Acts 3:10). Later, people were surprised by the boldness of Peter and John in teaching. Who is someone you know or have observed that you would describe as having "been with Jesus"? (Acts 4:13).

5. What are some ways you "teach and preach Jesus" daily? (Acts 5:42).

what is filling up my heart

NAME OF CHRIST _____

PONDER what it teaches about Him...

CONSIDER how He has shown up this way in your story... ♡

DISCOVER other scripture verses that mention or teach that same name

- •
- •

- •
- •

WHEN HAS THE SPIRIT...

ACTS 2

POURED OUT ...

FILLED UP ...

SPOKEN IN YOUR OWN LANGUAGE ...

CAUSED YOU TO ASK WHAT TO DO ...

SHOWN WONDERS ...

SAT UPON YOU ...

We can learn so much by watching the way that different people live the way of Jesus. What do you admire and observe from each of these ancient followers of Him? In what ways did Jesus make an impact in each of their stories?

1. What is the lesson you learn from Stephen?
(Acts 6—7).

2. What is the lesson you learn from Philip?
(Acts 8:26—40).

3. What is the lesson you learn from Saul?
(Acts 8:1—3; Acts 9:1—22).

4. What is the lesson you learn from Ananias?
(Acts 9:10—18).

5. What is the lesson you learn from Dorcas (Tabitha)?
(Acts 9:36—42).

INSIGHTS
& Impressions

NAME OF CHRIST

PONDER what it teaches about Him...

CONSIDER how He has shown up this way in your story... ♡

DISCOVER other scripture verses that mention or teach that same name

•

•

•

•

Acts 9

What Paul sees . . .

What God sees . . .

What Ananias sees . . .

What God sees . . .

What love looked like . . .

_____

_____

_____

Who is your Ananias?

_____

_____

Who is your Saul?

_____

_____

1. What do you learn from Cornelius and Peter about how the Spirit works? (Acts 10:1–18). What do you learn about God's power to coordinate and orchestrate?

2. What experiences in your life have taught you the most about revelation?

3. When has God answered a prayer that seemed unobtainable in a way that you were not expecting? What did you learn about Him and your relationship with Him? (Acts 12:1–17).

4. When has someone "stood round about" you when you were down? (Acts 14:19–20). What did you take with you from that experience? How might you strengthen and encourage someone to continue in their faith? (Acts 14:22).

5. How might you hazard your life for Christ today? (Acts 15:26).

Reflections

NAME OF CHRIST

PONDER what it teaches about Him...

CONSIDER how He has shown up this way in your story... ♡

DISCOVER other scripture verses that mention or teach that same name
-
-
-
-

PRINCIPLES of REVELATION

ACTS 11; ACTS 15:28

ACTS 11:5

ACTS 11:5

ACTS 15:28

ACTS 11:16-17

ACTS 11:6

ACTS 11:12, 15

ACTS 11:7

ACTS 11:11

ACTS 11:10

ACTS 11:8

1. Read Acts 17:22—31. What does Paul share with the people of Athens about the God he knows? What would you add to the list?

2. Read Acts 18:24—28. What do you love about Apollos? What scriptures would you choose to show Jesus is the Christ?

3. Read Acts 17:1—4, 10—12. What do you learn about opening your mind and heart to believe from Acts 17:11? What has that process looked like for you? Read Acts 19:13—15; Joseph Smith—History 1:20. In what ways do you think the adversary might view you as a threat?

4. Read Acts 16:13—15. What do you want to remember about Lydia? Read Acts 16:25—34. What do you learn about the keeper of the prison? How could you bring the words and messages of apostles to your household?

5. Read Acts 20:18—20, 30, 35—38. What do you see in these verses about Paul's style of ministering? How could you keep back nothing?

discoveries

NAME OF CHRIST

PONDER what it teaches about Him...

CONSIDER how He has shown up this way in your story... ♡

DISCOVER other scripture verses that mention or teach that same name

•   •

•   •

WHAT DO YOU KNOW ABOUT JESUS CHRIST?

ACTS 18:28

List your favorite scriptures about Him.

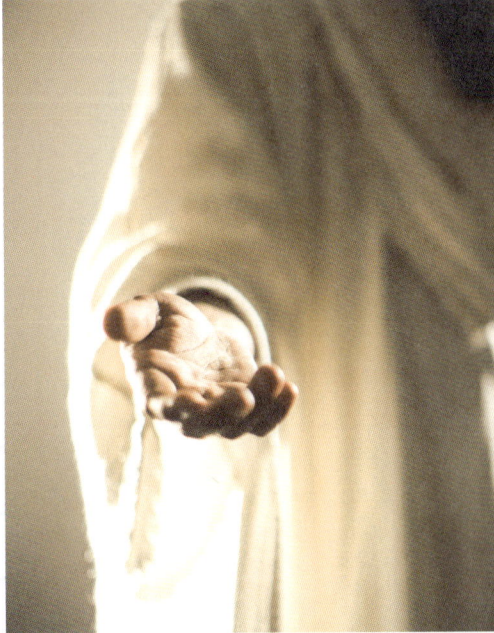

1. Read Acts 22:6–16. Paul is retelling his experience of meeting Jesus on the road to Damascus (see Acts 9). What do you learn about being a master teacher from Ananias?

2. Read Acts 23:11. The Lord stood by Paul and gave him a promise. What was the promise? Why would that have brought comfort to Paul? When has the Lord stood by you? Has He ever given you a promise that you still hold onto?

3. Read Acts 26:1–2, 19–29. What is the difference between being almost persuaded or altogether committed? Which one would you say you are?

4. Read Acts 27:25. How do you think Paul could still believe God even though he was in such dire circumstances? Is there something you can take from the story to help you strengthen your own belief in hard times?

5. Read Acts 28:1–6, 24 about the story of the viper. How do life circumstances sometimes affect our faith and belief? What would you teach the people of the island of Malta about believing despite our circumstance—good or bad?

A THING
OR TWO
I'VE LEARNED

NAME OF CHRIST

PONDER what it teaches about Him...

CONSIDER how He has shown up this way in your story... ♡

DISCOVER other scripture verses that mention or teach that same name
-
-
-
-

Anchor points...

Acts 27:23

Acts 27:24

Acts 27:25

Acts 27:26, 29

Acts 27:30-32

Acts 27:33-35

Acts 27:40

1. What is helpful background information to know about the book of Romans?

2. Read Romans 1:8, 12. How could sharing your faith increase and strengthen the faith of someone else? When have you seen faith actually make a difference?

3. Read Romans 3:22–26. Is there a place in your life where you feel you come short? How do you think God feels about your coming short—especially after you read verse 25 (including the footnotes)? Why do you think God designed *beforehand* for Christ to be a place of mercy?

4. Read Romans 4:16–21. Where is your hopeless place right now? Where are you barren? What can you not overcome? What do you learn about a God of hope from the story of Abraham?

5. Read Romans 5:20. Where is a place in your life where grace abounded more than weakness?

NAME OF CHRIST

PONDER what it teaches about Him…

CONSIDER how He has shown up this way in your story… ♡

DISCOVER other scripture verses that mention or teach that same name

-
-

-
-

Who do you know because of
their faith?
    Romans 1:8

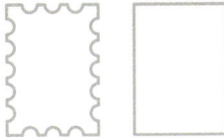

What could be spoken about
your faith?
    Romans 1:8

from _____
_____
_____
to _____
_____

What is one thing you believe about
the gospel?
    Romans 1:16

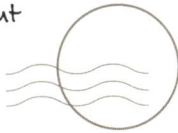

Why I am not ashamed of the gospel
of Christ...
    Romans 1:16

1. What role does the Spirit play in our prayers? See Romans 8:26. What impact do you think embracing this truth would have on your prayer life?

2. Read Romans 7:14–25; Romans 8:28–39. We all struggle with weakness and carnal things, but Christ has promised to help us conquer. List the phrases in these verses that give you courage and confidence as you work to overcome weak things.

3. What would it look like today to offer yourself as a living sacrifice? (Romans 12:1–2).

4. In the first few verses of Romans 16, we read about Phebe. Her description suggests that there was an ancient Relief Society of sorts, a group of women who believed "charity never faileth" (1 Corinthians 13:8). How might you be a succorer of many in your circle of influence right now?

5. Make a list of the heroes in Romans 16 and the kind things Paul said about each of them. Create your own list of heroes and write one kind thing about each of them. What good thing could the Savior say about you?

Things to
REMEMBER

NAME OF CHRIST ⌐──────────────┐
                 └──────────────┘

⌐**PONDER** what it ┐   ⌐**CONSIDER** how He ┐
teaches about Him...   has shown up this way
                        in your story... ♡

└   ┘   └   ┘

DISCOVER other scripture verses that mention
or teach that same name

•   •

•   •

a living sacrifice . . . holy, acceptable unto God

ROMANS 12

1. What do you learn about the Corinthians that would help you better understand the letters Paul wrote to them?

2. Read 1 Corinthians 3:6–7; 1 Corinthians 2:9.

- Who plants?

- Who waters?

- Who gives the increase?

- How would you encourage someone to better understand God's preparation and time frame?

3. Read 1 Corinthians 3:9–17. What thoughts and impressions do you have about becoming the temple of God?

4. If the kingdom of God is less about what we say and more about what we do, what will you do to help build the kingdom? (1 Corinthians 4:20–21).

5. This is a favorite Amish quote: "Does it ever occur to them that we aren't what we are because of the way we live, but rather we live as we do because of what we are? It comes from the inside out." How might housing the Holy Ghost change the way you live? (1 Corinthians 6:19–20).

CURRENTLY
THINKING
ABOUT

NAME OF CHRIST [_____]

PONDER what it teaches about Him...

CONSIDER how He has shown up this way in your story... ♡

DISCOVER other scripture verses that mention or teach that same name

- •
- •
- •
- •

Circle the materials you would use to build your house . . .

HAY

STUBBLE

GOLD

WOOD

PRECIOUS STONES

SILVER

What will the test be?

What part of your house will withstand the test?

What are your gold, silver, and precious stones?

SEE 1 CORINTHIANS 3:9-17

1. Read 1 Corinthians 9:1–3, 10—14. What four things would you find in Paul if you were to examine him?

   ○

   ○

   ○

   ○

Are those four things found in you? Why might you want them to be?

2. What do you learn from Paul about meeting people where they are as they are—especially as you lead and teach? (1 Corinthians 9:19—24).

3. When you are tempted above that which ye are able, what does a faithful God promise to do? (1 Corinthians 10:13).

4. List the spiritual gifts found in 1 Corinthians 12, then add to your list some spiritual gifts that are not found in chapter 12. What are your gifts? How are you using them to profit others? (1 Corinthians 12:7).

5. Why is charity the ultimate gift, and why does it never fail? (1 Corinthians 13).

MEMORABLE

NAME OF CHRIST _____

PONDER what it teaches about Him...

CONSIDER how He has shown up this way in your story... ♡

DISCOVER other scripture verses that mention or teach that same name

-
-

What does God see in you?

What do others see in you?

1. Faith communities can be places where we gather to find strength, encouragement, or comfort. How has gathering with fellow believers had an impact for good on you? (1 Corinthians 14:3).

2. There are many significant voices in the world today. Which of those give an uncertain sound? Which are helping you prepare to battle? (1 Corinthians 14:8—10).

3. Have you ever felt like the least? How has God been able to make you more than what you thought you could achieve? (1 Corinthians 15:9—10).

4. We can strive to be steadfast, unmovable, always abounding in the work, but we must remember that the _____ is in Christ (1 Corinthians 15:57). How does that change the way you view your day-to-day efforts?

5. Read 1 Corinthians 16:6—7.

"And _____ that I will abide, yea, and winter with you, that ye may bring me on my journey _____ I go. For I will not see you now by the way; but _____ _____ to tarry a while with you, _____ the Lord permit."

What do you learn from these words about what it looks like to live a surrendered life?

what is filling up my heart

NAME OF CHRIST

PONDER what it teaches about Him...

CONSIDER how He has shown up this way in your story... ♡

DISCOVER other scripture verses that mention or teach that same name

•

•

•

•

"Do all in your power to prepare the hearts of men so the Spirit can teach."

See Gene R. Cook, "Inviting Others to Come unto Christ," *Ensign*, November 1988.

PRAY

USE THE SCRIPTURES

TESTIFY

USE MUSIC

EXPRESS LOVE & GRATITUDE

SHARE SPIRITUAL EXPERIENCES

PARTICIPATE IN PRIESTHOOD ORDINANCES

LET all THINGS be DONE unto EDIFYING

When ye come together, every one of you hath a psalm, hath a doctrine, hath a tongue, hath a revelation, hath an interpretation.

1 CORINTHIANS 14:26

1. When has God been the Father of mercies and the God of all comfort for you? (2 Corinthians 1:3).

2. Read 2 Corinthians 2:12–14; 2 Corinthians 7:5–7. When has God sent a "Titus" to you in a time of trouble? What did that person do to help you?

3. How can you be the living epistle of Christ? (2 Corinthians 3:3).

4. How has God gotten rid of old things and brought new things into your life? (2 Corinthians 5:17). Why do you think God wants to be involved in your story?

5. Read Corinthians 6:1–10, 16–18. Why would these promises be the means of perfecting holiness in someone?

everything
I'm soaking in

NAME OF CHRIST

PONDER what it teaches about Him...

CONSIDER how He has shown up this way in your story... ♡

DISCOVER other scripture verses that mention or teach that same name

-
-

-
-

Help to get through the heavy things from
"the Father of **mercies**, and the God of all **comfort**"
(2 Corinthians 1:3-4).

1. How does God know you love Him? How do others know? What is the proof of your love? (2 Corinthians 8).

2. What might it look like to be "ready now"? (2 Corinthians 9:1–8).

3. What is Christ's measure for you right now? (2 Corinthians 10:13).

4. Have you ever met a man or woman in Christ? How did he or she bless your life? (2 Corinthians 12:2).

5. Examine yourself. Is Jesus Christ in you? In what ways? Is your life ready for inspection? (2 Corinthians 13:5).

INSIGHTS & Impressions

NAME OF CHRIST

PONDER what it teaches about Him...

CONSIDER how He has shown up this way in your story... ♡

DISCOVER other scripture verses that mention or teach that same name
-
-
-
-

EXAMINE yourself...

DO I GIVE OF MY ABUNDANCE? 2 Cor. 8:14 ------------------------------

----

AM I A FELLOWHELPER? 2 Cor. 8:23 ------------------------------

----

WHAT'S THE PROOF OF MY LOVE? 2 Cor. 8:24 --------------------

----

AM I READY NOW? 2 Cor. 9:3 ------------------------------------

----

AM I A CHEERFUL GIVER? 2 Cor. 9:7 -----------------------------

----

DO I LOOK ON THINGS OUTWARD OR BY GOD'S MEASURE? 2 Cor. 10:7

AM I IN THE FAITH? 2 Cor. 13:5 --------------------------------

----

AM I PROGRESSING? 2 Cor. 13:11 --------------------------------

----

AM I AN ENCOURAGER? 2 Cor. 13:11 ------------------------------

----

AM I A UNIFIER? 2 Cor. 13:11 ----------------------------------

----

AM I A MAN OR WOMAN IN CHRIST? 2 Cor. 12:2 -------------------

----

What do you learn about the Galatian Saints that would help you better appreciate this letter? Galatians is the book that teaches about the fruits of the Spirit and how Christ lives in us. Consider those two things as you learn about living in faith.

1. What does it look like to live in love and joy? (Galatians 5:14; 6:2, 10; 4:6–7, 28).

2. How might you live in peace and longsuffering? (Galatians 6:16; 4:4).

3. What do you learn about gentleness and goodness? (Galatians 4:12, 18; 6:4, 9–10).

4. What are the marks of a man or woman filled with meekness and temperance? (Galatians 5:1, 7, 24; 6:1).

5. How do all of these characteristics help you to bear the marks of Christ? (Galatians 6:17).

inspiration

NAME OF CHRIST

PONDER what it teaches about Him...

CONSIDER how He has shown up this way in your story... ♡

DISCOVER other scripture verses that mention or teach that same name

-
-

-
-

When was a time I have seen this **fruit** in me?

temperance

LOVE

joy

PEACE

longsuffering

GENTLENESS

GOODNESS

FAITH

meekness

Galatians 5:22-23

1. What is important to know about Ephesians? When you consider the work of gathering together all things in one, what does that mean for *all* of us and also for *each* of us? (Ephesians 1:10).

2. How is grace a gift both in salvation and in exaltation? (Ephesians 2:4—10).

3. What was Paul teaching the Ephesians about the value of having apostles and prophets? (Ephesians 4:11—14).

4. How have other Saints helped you to comprehend and know the breadth, length, depth, and height of the love of Christ? (Ephesians 3:17—21).

5. It seems Ephesians 6:13—18 prepares you for a frontal attack. Who has your back? (see Isaiah 52:12; 58:8).

Reflections

NAME OF CHRIST

PONDER what it teaches about Him...

CONSIDER how He has shown up this way in your story... ♡

DISCOVER other scripture verses that mention or teach that same name

-
-

-
-

PUT ON THE WHOLE ARMOR OF GOD...

EPHESIANS 6:11-18

ISAIAH 52:12

1. What do you want to remember about Philippians and Colossians as you read Paul's counsel to them? Read Philippians 2:6, 12–13. Describe the synergy between working out our salvation and God working in us.

2. Read Philippians 3:8–10 and Colossians 3:12–24. What does the process of coming to know Christ include? Make a list of how these verses might help us in our hope to become more like Him.

3. When has Christ strengthened you to do something you wouldn't have been able to do on your own? (Philippians 4:13).

4. What are the descriptions for what it might look like to become complete in Christ? (see Colossians 1:23; 2:10).

-
-
-
-

5. How does Paul describe the people who are on the journey toward Christ with him? (Colossians 4). How would you describe the people who are on the journey with you?

A
place
for
thoughts...

NAME OF CHRIST

PONDER what it teaches about Him...

CONSIDER how He has shown up this way in your story... ♡

DISCOVER other scripture verses that mention or teach that same name

-
-

-
-

PRISON SENTENCES

Rejoice again
I say Rejoice

Philippians 4:4

I can do
all things through
Christ which
Strengtheneth me

Philippians 4:13

The Lord is
at hand

Philippians 4:5

1. What do you learn about the book of Thessalonians? What advice does Paul give in 1 Thessalonians 2:7–20 about how to minister in a godly manner?

2. Look for phrases in 1 Thessalonians 3 and 4 about how to perfect your faith. Write them here.

3. Read the list in 1 Thessalonians 5:14–23. What might you look for in the process and path of becoming sanctified and holy?

4. Read 1 Thessalonians 5:1–10 and 2 Thessalonians 2:1–12. What do you learn from these verses that would help you to not be shaken?

5. What is the difference between a busybody (to bustle about, work all around) and someone with quiet confidence? Which one are you hoping to become? (2 Thessalonians 3:11–13).

discoveries

NAME OF CHRIST

PONDER what it teaches about Him...

CONSIDER how He has shown up this way in your story... ♡

DISCOVER other scripture verses that mention or teach that same name

-
-

-
-

1 THESSALONIANS 5:11-23

REJOICE EVERMORE

COMFORT YOURSELVES TOGETHER

PRAY WITHOUT CEASING

HOLD FAST THAT WHICH IS GOOD

IN EVERY THING GIVE THANKS

PROVE ALL THINGS

QUENCH NOT THE SPIRIT

1. What do you learn about the letters to Timothy, Titus, and Philemon? Read 1 Timothy 4:14; 2 Timothy 1:5–6; 3:14–17. What is your gift? Who has stirred it up in you?

2. Read 2 Timothy 3:1–7 and then read 1 Timothy 4:1–13. What does it look like to live as a believer, particularly during the last days?

3. Read 2 Timothy 4:1–17 and 1 Timothy 6:11–21. What encourages and enables you to fight a good fight and keep the faith?

4. Read Titus 2:1–8. If you could give one piece of spiritual advice to the younger you, what would it be?

5. What have you done for love's sake? (Philemon).

So good

NAME OF CHRIST

PONDER what it teaches about Him...

CONSIDER how He has shown up this way in your story... ♡

DISCOVER other scripture verses that mention or teach that same name
- •
- •
- •
- •

Grace to you...

Jesus

Who would Jesus ask you to love well right now?
— Philemon

1. Read Hebrews 3:14. What do you think it means to "hold the beginning of [your] confidence steadfast unto the end"?

2. In what ways has God borne witness to you with signs, wonders, miracles, and gifts? (Hebrews 2:4).

3. What is one of your favorite names of Christ from these chapters?

4. Christ's mortal experience gave Him a unique ability to understand us and succor us (Hebrews 2:18). Why and how does that knowledge encourage you to "come boldly unto the throne of grace"? (Hebrews 4:16).

5. How have the promises of Jesus Christ become an anchor to your soul? Which ones in particular? (Hebrews 6:19–20).

A THING
OR TWO
I'VE LEARNED

NAME OF CHRIST _____

PONDER what it teaches about Him...

CONSIDER how He has shown up this way in your story... ♡

DISCOVER other scripture verses that mention or teach that same name
-
-
-
-

WORKS
OF
CHRIST

....

....

....

....

....

....

....

....

ATTRIBUTES
OF
CHRIST

....

....

....

....

....

....

....

....

....

....

TITLES
OF
CHRIST

....

....

....

....

....

....

....

....

....

....

Hebrews 1—6

1. Where have you seen Christ as the High Priest of Good Things to Come in your story? (Hebrews 9:11—12).

2. Read Hebrews 10:19—39. How does this list of verses help convince you to cast not away your confidence or to draw back?

3. From Hebrews 11, what do you learn faith is? Give a definition.

4. What does an author do? What is the work of a finisher (such as a finish carpenter)? How has Jesus been an author and finisher for you? (Hebrews 12:2).

5. Read Hebrews 13:1—2; Exodus 23:9; Matthew 25: 35. What does it look like to live the hospitality code?

NAME OF CHRIST

PONDER what it teaches about Him...

CONSIDER how He has shown up this way in your story... ♡

DISCOVER other scripture verses that mention or teach that same name

-
-

-
-

believing big

Hebrews 12:1-3

my cloud of witnesses

1. What do you learn about the background of the book of James? What is trying your faith right now? What do you need to ask God? (James 1:1–5).

2. Read James 1:27 and 2:1–8. When have you seen someone live the royal law?

3. When we discuss faith and works, we sometimes debate if faith *or* works is more important. What if the *or* is wrong? What if this is not an "either/or" but rather a "both/and" situation? Why do we need both faith and works? How does this way of living make us a friend to God? (see James 2:14–17, 23).

4. The book of James is full of sticky statements— powerful one-liners such as "every good gift . . . cometh down from the Father of lights" (James 1:17). What do you love about this simple statement? Can you find more sticky statements?

5. What advice does James give for the rougher, trying patches of life? (James 5:16).

write ***that down!***

NAME OF CHRIST

PONDER what it teaches about Him...

CONSIDER how He has shown up this way in your story... ♡

DISCOVER other scripture verses that mention or teach that same name

STICKY STATEMENTS
FROM THE BOOK OF JAMES

Live the royal law

JAMES 1:8

Let patience have her work

JAMES 1:4

1. Read 1 Peter 1:6—9. Why and how is a trial of faith more precious than gold?

2. Why do you believe Jesus Christ is precious? (1 Peter 2:7).

3. How could you love life and *SEE* a good day today? (1 Peter 3:10).

4. Think of the process of becoming in 2 Peter 1:5—8. Which one are you practicing right now?

5. When have you been an eyewitness of His majesty? (2 Peter 1:16).

Things I don't want to forget . . .

NAME OF CHRIST

PONDER what it teaches about Him...

CONSIDER how He has shown up this way in your story... ♡

DISCOVER other scripture verses that mention or teach that same name
-
-
-
-

WHO IS SOMEONE YOU KNOW who is FILLED WITH...

DILIGENCE _____

FAITH _____

VIRTUE _____

KNOWLEDGE _____

TEMPERANCE _____

PATIENCE _____

GODLINESS _____

BROTHERLY KINDNESS _____

CHARITY _____

*Whereby are given unto us exceeding great and precious promises:
that by these ye might be partakers of the divine nature . . .*

2 PETER 1:4

1. What do you learn about the epistles of John and Jude? What are the stages of spiritual maturity? (1 John 2:12–14).

2. If we are of God and God is love, then what should our lives in God look like? (1 John 4:6, 8).

3. What gives us confidence in prayer? (1 John 5:14–15).

4. Read Jude 1:16–25. What is the difference between the mockers and the beloved?

5. Read 2 John. What have you learned from another person's faith that helped to strengthen yours?

Things to
REMEMBER

NAME OF CHRIST [_____]

PONDER what it teaches about Him...

CONSIDER how He has shown up this way in your story... ♡

DISCOVER other scripture verses that mention or teach that same name

- •
- •

- •
- •

What Love Looked Like.

Beloved, let us love one another: for love is of God; and every one that loveth is born of God, and knoweth God.

1 John 4:7

DATE	LOCATION	WHAT LOVE LOOKED LIKE

1. What are the themes of the book of Revelation?

2. Rewrite the symbolic description of Jesus found in Revelation 1:12–18.

3. Consider your situation right now. What could the Lord commend you for? What counsel do you think He might share with you? What promise do you need from Him right now? (Revelation 2–3).

4. The address to every church begins by describing a symbolic description of Christ. Which is your favorite description? Why?

5. What reasons do you have to give glory, honor, and thanks to God? (Revelation 4:9).

what is filling up my heart

NAME OF CHRIST

PONDER what it teaches about Him...

CONSIDER how He has shown up this way in your story... ♡

DISCOVER other scripture verses that mention or teach that same name

- •
- •

- •
- •

∶○∶ LEADING WITH HOPE ∶○∶

Come up hither
24

HOPE IN [   ]
· Revelation 4-5 ·

DAN SWIFTEST 4:4

JASPER
LIFE
JUSTICE
FIRST

SARDINE
DEATH
MERCY
LAST

JUDAH
NOBLEST
4:7

EPHRAIM
STRONGEST
4:7

4:4

4:3 RAINBOW: COVENANT OF ETERNAL LIFE

REUBEN
WISEST
4:7

HOLY! HOLY! HOLY!
GLORY! HONOR! POWER!

THE COVENANT PURPOSE

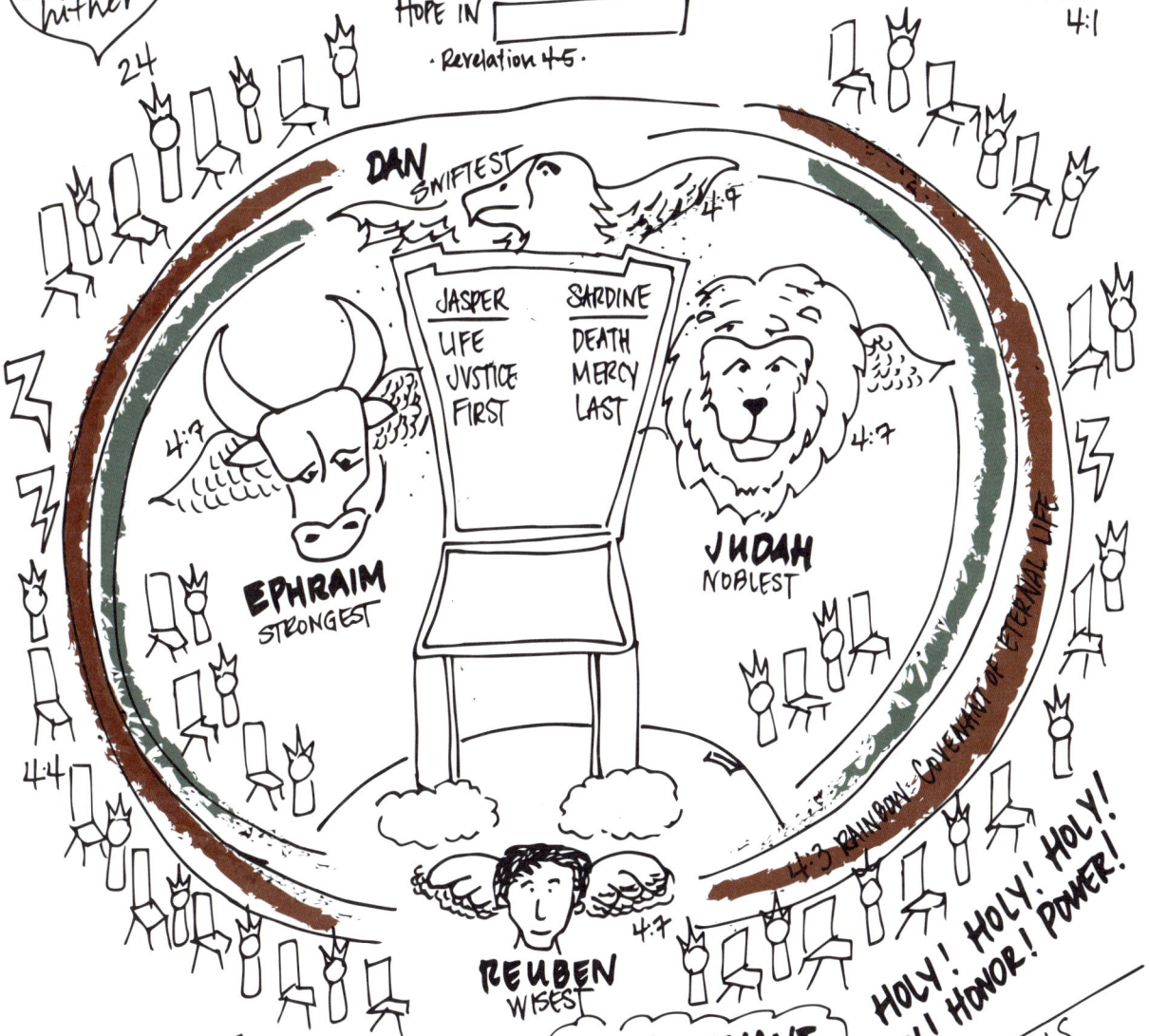

OPENING THE SCROLL: _____ 5:1

WORTHY: _____

What did John hear? (5:5)
What did John see? (5:6)
Seven horns:
Seven eyes:
Slain:
Lamb mentioned [ ] times

1. _____
   4:11, 5:8

2. _____
   5:9-11

3. _____
   5:12

SYMBOLS
Gold:
Crown:
3:
24:
7:
EYES:
WINGS:
RAINBOW:
THRONE:

1. What happened in each of these seals?

    • 1000

    • 2000

    • 3000

    • 4000

    • 5000

    • 6000

    • 7000

2. Who will be able to stand? (Revelation 7).

3. What do you learn about Zerubbabel? (Zechariah 4).
What do you learn about Joshua? (Zechariah 3). Why
do restoration and gathering play such an important
part in God's plan of hope?

4. Where do you see a valley of decision battle raging
today? (Revelation 12 and 14).

5. How have you taken His mark upon you? How
do you express your devotion? (Revelation 7:3;
13:16—18).

CURRENTLY
THINKING
ABOUT

NAME OF CHRIST

PONDER what it teaches about Him...

CONSIDER how He has shown up this way in your story... ♡

DISCOVER other scripture verses that mention or teach that same name
-
-
-
-

The valley of decision

JOEL 3:14

Write evidence of the dragon, the beast, and Babylon

Write evidence of God, His Christ, and His kingdom

How the battle was won

REVELATION 12:11

MEMORABLE

NAME OF CHRIST [   ]

PONDER what it teaches about Him...

CONSIDER how He has shown up this way in your story... ♡

DISCOVER other scripture verses that mention or teach that same name

-
-

-
-

1. How do you remain called, chosen, and faithful during a battle for souls? (Revelation 17:14).

2. In what areas of your life do you hear the call, "Come out of her"? How will you respond? (Revelation 18:4).

3. Look back over all the names of Christ we studied this year. What name would you call Him? (Revelation 19:11–12).

4. What tears do you need the Lord to wipe away? Why does it give you hope to know there will be no more tears over what you cried for in mortality? (Revelation 21:4).

5. What have you learned this year about Jesus Christ that makes you wish He would come quickly? (Revelation 22:20).

discoveries

NAME OF CHRIST

PONDER what it teaches about Him...

CONSIDER how He has shown up this way in your story... ♡

DISCOVER other scripture verses that mention or teach that same name

-
-

-
-

Surely I come quickly. Amen. Even so, come, Lord Jesus.

REVELATION 22:20

Using all that you have learned about Jesus Christ, along with
Revelation 21-22, write what makes you so excited
for Jesus to come again.

write
that
down!